It Gets Better

A Book of Healing

By Amber Huntington Wright

Photography by Sarah Wood

Dedicated to the Sandy Hook Elementary School community

At one point or another, all of us have been hurt. These moments are scary at the beginning, painful in the middle, but are overcome in the end. As you find your way back to joy, know that

it gets better.

Sometimes,
you may feel as though your heart is broken into tiny pieces, but *it gets better.*

Hearts can be mended by love.

Sometimes,
you may have bad dreams that keep
you up at night, but
it gets better.

There are many people and things to help comfort you.

Sometimes,
you may feel bad for a friend who lost their life when you didn't, but

it gets better.

Remember that they are happy and in a safe and beautiful place. They want you to be happy too.

Sometimes,
you may feel that the things you saw and heard keep coming up in your mind whether you want them to or not, but *it gets better.*

8

After your mind sorts everything out, the bad memories can be replaced with good things. It is important to take time and let yourself heal on the inside.

Sometimes,
you may be scared to go places and
be afraid of strangers you meet, but

it gets better.

The world is still a happy place with many good and caring people.

Sometimes,
you may wish and wish that it never happened; then you are reminded that it did, but *it gets better.*

After a while, as you love and care for others, the hurt goes away.

Sometimes,
you may feel that it is hard to be happy or even to have fun, but

it gets better.

Friends and family will always be there to cheer you up. Together you can try new, fun things.

Sometimes,
you may feel like crying even when
it seems there are no tears left, but

it gets better.

Crying is okay. It will help you heal, and it shows how much you really care. When you have worked through your feelings you don't need to cry as much.

Sometimes,
you may believe your life isn't good anymore, but

it gets better.

You will start to feel stronger than you were before and even discover new and amazing things about yourself.

Sometimes,
you may feel that you don't want to get out of bed or do anything, but

it gets better.

Some days are just like that, and it's okay. Just remember there are still many happy days ahead.

Sometimes,
you may feel alone, and different than you were before. You may think you will never feel normal again, but

it gets much better.

Remember that your hopes and dreams are important, and your friends and family will help you give them life again.

Sometimes,
bad things may happen to you. Those things don't have to determine who you are. You were meant for more. Bad experiences, as well as the good ones, can be stepping-stones to a better and brighter future. Healing takes time, but it will get better. You will find your way. You will succeed. You can be strong. You are loved. And **you will heal.**

it gets much better.

Special Thanks
to my husband Briton Wright
to the generous people who supported this project on GoFundMe.com
to Kathy Carlston for her layout work and design
to Liz Carlston for bringing this project to fruition

About the Author

Amber Huntington Wright is an elementary school teacher and also a survivor of the Columbine High School shooting. She is passionate about helping people heal and recover from tragic events. Amber is the mother of an adorable boy and lives in American Fork, Utah, with her husband, Briton.

About the Photographer

Sarah Wood is a photographer with a talent for finding and capturing the beauty of every day life. She has a passion for framing time and holding on to the ever fleeting moments of life through pictures and spends most of her time behind a camera. She lives in American Fork, Utah and has a wonderful husband, four beautiful children, and an adorable schnauzer named Walter. See her work at:
www.photographybyrememberwhen.com

To watch videos and learn more visit: www.ResilientHope.org

Contact us at: ItGetsBetterBook@gmail.com